STEP-UP Books

are written especially for children who have outgrown beginning readers. In this exciting series:

- the words are harder (but not too hard)
- there's more text (but it's still in big print)
- there are plenty of illustrations (but the books aren't picture books)
- the subject matter has been carefully chosen to appeal to young readers who want to find out about the world around them. They'll love these informative and lively books.

MAGICIANS DO AMAZING THINGS

How did
- Houdini "walk through" a brick wall?
- Harry Kellar cause a princess to "float" in the air?
- Chung Ling Soo "catch" live goldfish from thin air?

Find the answers to these and three other baffling tricks in this fascinating collection of true stories about some of the world's greatest magicians.

MAGICIANS

by Robert Kraske

Do Amazing Things

illustrated by Richard Bennett

Step-Up Books

Random House • New York

Library of Congress Cataloging in Publication Data Kraske, Robert. Magicians Do Amazing Things. (Step-Up books; 27) CONTENTS: The Indian basket trick.—The trickiest trick.—The Chinese wizard. [etc.]
1. Conjuring—Juvenile literature. 2. Magicians—Juvenile literature. [1. Magic tricks. 2. Magicians] I. Title GV1548.K7 793.8'092'2 [B] 78-64640 ISBN 0-394-84106-9 ISBN 0-394-94106-3 lib. bdg.
Manufactured in the United States of America   1 2 3 4 5 6 7 8 9 0

Contents

The Indian Basket Trick

Raymond Saunders was a famous American magician. He called himself The Great Raymond. He traveled all over the world to find new tricks for his magic show.

Raymond went to India in the year 1912. In a village he met a poor magician standing under a big tree.

"See the greatest magic act in all the

world!" the magician called. He waved a sword so that people passing by would look at him. "My father performed this wonder! My FATHER'S FATHER performed this wonder! Your eyes have never seen such a marvel!"

The magician wore a white turban and a black vest. Around his hips hung a red cloth like a skirt. A small boy stood beside him, smiling. A large basket stood on the ground.

People stopped. They listened to the magician. Then they looked at the boy and the large basket.

Raymond had watched magicians in many large cities. A poor magician in a small village in India could not fool him! After all, he was The Great Raymond! He had given magic shows in Paris and New York. In England he had performed before the king.

Raymond thought about walking on. But he was tired. The shade of the big tree felt cool.

"One penny!" the magician called. "One penny to see this greatest of all magic acts!" People placed pennies in his thin hand. Raymond gave him a coin.

The magician stepped behind the basket. "Now watch closely. You will not believe what your eyes see!"

The boy stepped into the basket and sat down. The magician placed the cover on the basket. He held his arms up to the sky. He said words that Raymond did not understand. Then he took the cloth from around his waist and held it in front of the basket. He said more strange words. Again he wrapped the cloth around his waist.

The magician held up the sword and showed it to the people. Then, quickly, he plunged it into the basket! Once, twice, three times! The people heard the boy scream, "Ayy! Ayy!" And finally, "Ohhh . . ." No other sound came from inside the basket.

Slowly, the magician drew the sword from the basket. He held it up to the people. It was dripping with blood!

The people gasped.

"What have you done to the boy?" they said. "If you have killed him. . .!"

"Wait!" the magician cried. He bent down and slowly lifted the lid. The crowd came close to look inside. Then they began talking in excited voices and pointing.

THE BASKET WAS EMPTY!

Raymond was amazed. He had seen thousands of tricks. But never one like this!

"The boy!" people were crying. "Where is he? What have you done with him?"

Just then, Raymond heard a yell. Everyone looked up. There was the boy! He was sitting on a branch of the big shade tree. He was smiling and swinging his legs.

Raymond could hardly believe his eyes. "I must have that trick!" he thought. "I must have it for my magic show."

The people
moved away. The
boy climbed down
from the tree. Raymond
went up to the magician.
"I know who you are," the
magician said. "You are The
Great Raymond."

Raymond was pleased to
hear this. "I would very much
like to buy that trick
from you," he
said. "With it,
I could amaze
people all over
the world."

The magician agreed to sell the trick. Raymond paid the price he asked. "Now, tell me how you did it," Raymond said.

The magician looked around. He wanted to make sure no one could hear what he was about to say. Then he whispered into Raymond's ear.

Raymond listened. He looked at the sword red with blood. His eyes went to the grinning boy standing beside the magician. Slowly his face broke into a smile. "So THAT'S how you did it. How simple!"

The magician stepped back. He looked at Raymond. "Simple?" he said. "Yes, the trick IS simple. But only AFTER I told you how to do it. Otherwise, you never would have guessed."

Can YOU guess what the magician told Raymond? Think about it. Then read the solution on page 50.

The Trickiest Trick

"The trickiest trick that ever tricked a New York audience!"

That is what *The World Magazine* said about Harry Houdini's new trick. He performed it the first time on the night of Monday, July 13, 1914. The theater was in New York. It was called Hammerstein's Roof Garden.

Houdini was one of the world's best magicians. Mostly he did escape tricks. He escaped from a bank safe, from a wooden box under water, and from jail cells. But he also did other kinds of tricks.

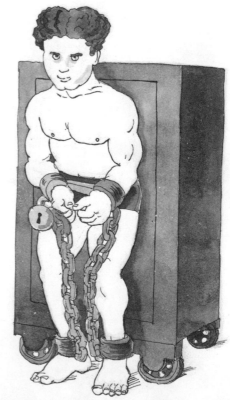

From the Roof Garden stage he told the audience, "I have a new trick to show you. Tonight you will see me do the impossible. I will walk through a brick wall!"

People in the audience said, "Ha! Who could ever walk through a wall!"

The stage was empty except for a large rug. "We are going to build a wall on this rug," Houdini said.

He clapped his hands—once, twice. Workmen rolled out a long piece of steel, a beam. It was on small wheels. They rolled the beam onto the rug. Then they began building a brick wall on the beam.

Houdini stood at the front of the stage. "I need thirty men," he said. "Who will come onstage and watch me?"

By chance, another magician was in the audience. His name was Saram Ellison. He was a member of the Society of American Magicians, a club of magicians in New York.

"I will go onto the stage," he said. "Just let Houdini try to fool me!" Ellison and 29 other men went onto the stage.

The workmen finished the wall. It stood about nine feet high and ten feet long.

"Is the wall strong?" Houdini asked the people on stage. "Is it solid?"

All 30 men felt the wall. They tapped it
with a workman's hammer. "It is a real brick
wall," they told the audience.

Houdini asked the men to form a half
circle around the wall. He clapped his hands

again. His helpers carried two screens onto
the stage. They placed one screen on one
side of the wall. Just its edges touched the
bricks. They placed the second screen on the
other side of the wall.

"Everyone watch," Houdini called. "I will now walk through a brick wall!"

Ellison whispered to the people on the stage, "Keep your eyes open. Houdini will now try to trick us."

The audience could see the front end of the wall and the two screens. The people onstage could see the back end of the wall and the two screens. Everyone could see the top of the wall. It stood about three feet higher than the screens.

Houdini opened one screen, stepped inside, and closed it around him. The screen hid him from everyone. "Here I am," he called. He waved his hands above the screen. "Now I'm going . . . I'm going . . . I'm gone!"

Helpers quickly took the screen from the wall. Houdini was not there. He had disappeared!

The helpers
walked around the
wall. They took
away the second
screen.

There was
Houdini on the
other side of the
wall. He smiled
and bowed.

"Impossible!"
people said. "Houdini
walked right through a brick wall!"

The people on the stage went up to the
wall. They looked closely at it. Not a brick
was out of place. The wall was as solid as
when it was made. "How did he do it?" they
asked.

"I'm puzzled," Ellison said. "The answer is beyond me. Houdini didn't go over the wall. We would have seen him. He didn't pull out bricks from the wall. It would have fallen down. He could not go under the wall. It's too near the floor. Besides, we were standing on the rug. It didn't move. Houdini must have gone through the wall! But how? Only one person knows the secret—Houdini himself!"

How did Houdini get from one side of the wall to the other? How did he fool Ellison and all the people in the theater? Hundreds of eyes watched him. But no one saw what he did.

Did he fool you, too? Or do you know how he did it? Check your answer with the solution on page 53.

The Chinese Wizard

People came early to the Alhambra Theatre in London, England. They wanted to see Chung Ling Soo. Newspapers called him the "Chinese wizard."

The curtain opened. The people saw a tall man. A braid of hair hung down the back of his head. He wore a long red and yellow robe. From one sleeve, he pulled a white cloth. He held the cloth near the stage. Then he took it away. There stood a large fishbowl! It was filled with water.

"Did you see that!" people said. "That must be Chinese magic!"

Next a pretty, young Chinese woman came onto the stage. She also wore a robe. Her hair had two braids, one around each ear. She wore a rose in each braid. She carried a long fishing pole.

"I am Suee Seen," she told the people. "Master Chung speaks no English. So I will speak for him. He wants to do a special mystery for you. This mystery has never been seen outside China. Do you see this empty bowl of water? Master Chung will fill the bowl with goldfish. Where will he get the goldfish? Watch!"

A man whispered to a friend. "I know where the fish are. UP THE SLEEVES OF HIS ROBE! Look at those sleeves. You could drive a bus into them!"

It seemed the Chinese magician knew
what the audience was thinking. He folded
back the sleeves. Now his arms were bare.

Suee Seen gave Chung Ling Soo a fishing
pole. A hook was at the end of the fishing
line. On the hook, he placed a piece of bait.
The bait looked like an inch-long worm.

"Now Master Chung will go fishing,"
Suee Seen said. "Will he catch anything?
Let us see."

The Chinese magician held the pole over
the heads of the people in the first few rows.
Slowly he waved it back and forth. The
people watched closely. Then the magician
swung the pole up. On the end of the hook
was a goldfish. It shone in the light.

Chung Ling Soo swung the line in. He
took the fish off the hook. He dropped it
into the bowl. It swam around and around.

Suee Seen placed more bait on the hook.
Again the magician waved the pole over the
audience. Then he swung it up. Another
goldfish was on the line.

Chung Ling Soo placed the second fish with the first one in the bowl. Then he went on to catch six more fish in the air above the people's heads.

People wondered how he did it.

"Suee Seen must place the fish on the hook."

"No, no. The fish ALWAYS appear in the air. She does not touch them."

"He made the fishbowl appear from nowhere, didn't he? That is where he got the goldfish. From NOWHERE! He really is a Chinese wizard!"

Where did the goldfish come from? And the bowl? Were these old Chinese mysteries? Or were they very clever tricks? What do you say? For the solution, turn to page 56.

The Floating Princess

The poster outside the theater read:

TONIGHT — 8 P.M.
HARRY KELLAR
SEE THE MARVEL
OF THE
FLOATING PRINCESS

On the poster was a drawing of Kellar. A man and a woman stood looking at it.

"Kellar has a bald head," said the man. "Just like my uncle."

The woman said, "He does not LOOK like a magician. I don't think he could fool anyone."

That is what many people said about Harry Kellar. But Kellar was one of the best magicians of the early 1900s. Another magician once said, "On the stage, Kellar does miracles!"

"The Floating Princess" was one of his very special "miracles."

People in the theater saw a young woman on the stage. She was lying on a sofa. She wore the costume of a princess from India. Her name was Princess Karnac.

". . . nine . . . eight . . . seven . . . six . . ." Kellar slowly counted as he hypnotized the princess. "You are falling into a deep sleep. Five . . . four . . . three . . . two . . . one. . . .

Now you are sleeping . . . sleeping . . . a deep . . . deep . . . sleep. . . ."

Kellar turned to the people.

"Ladies and gentlemen. For hundreds of years, magicians in India have made people float in mid-air. After years of travel and study, I, Harry Kellar, have discovered the great secret. Watch!"

Kellar stepped over to the woman on the sofa. He waved his hands above her.

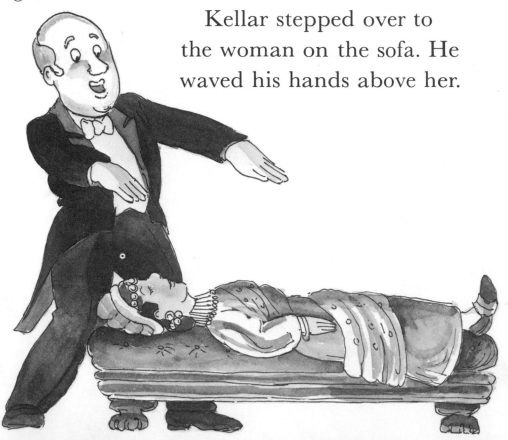

"Up!" he commanded.

For a moment, nothing happened.
Princess Karnac stayed on the sofa. Then
slowly she began to rise . . . up . . . up. Soon
she was six feet in the air.

Kellar pulled away the sofa. There was
nothing under the princess.

"Impossible!" people said. "She is floating
in mid-air!"

A helper gave Kellar a large hoop about
five feet wide. Kellar showed it to people in
the first row.

"Please feel the hoop," he said. "Is it one
piece? Make sure there are no spaces in it."

The people felt it. They looked at it
closely. "Yes," they said. "The hoop is all in
one piece."

"Then watch!" Kellar said.

Kellar went to the floating princess.

He placed the hoop over her head. Slowly
he walked to her feet. The hoop passed
along the woman's body. Then he walked
the hoop back to her head.

Kellar then placed the hoop over the woman's feet. He walked it up to her head. The people saw the hoop pass again along her body. NOTHING WAS HOLDING HER UP!

Kellar gave the hoop to his helper. He pulled the sofa back under the princess.

He held up his hands. Slowly he lowered them. Gently, the woman floated down . . . down . . . . Then she rested on the sofa. Kellar clapped his hands once . . . twice . . . three times. The princess blinked. She sat up.

Kellar turned to the people and bowed. They clapped and cheered. They were amazed at what they had seen. A woman floating in mid-air!

Did Kellar perform a miracle? Did he really make the princess float in mid-air? What is your guess? For the answer, turn to page 60.

The Iron Box in the Orange Tree

A messenger stood at the door. "I bring a letter from King Louis Philippe," he said. "It is for Jean-Eugène Robert-Houdin" (zhon oo-ZHEN roe-BARE oo-DAN). The year was 1846.

"Look at this!" the great French magician said. "The king commands me to put on a show at the Palace of St. Cloud."

"Papa," his son Emile (ay-MEAL) said. "Is there a new trick you can do? The king has seen all your magic shows. He will expect something special."

"I have been thinking of a new trick," Robert-Houdin said. "It is one the king has never seen before." He smiled at Emile. "And you, my son, will help me."

At St. Cloud one week later, the king and his friends waited for the show to begin. They saw a fireplace and two tables on a stage. One table was in the middle of the stage. The second table was at the side of the stage. On this table was a bell-shaped cover made of cloudy glass. No one could see through it. A candle holder stood on the fireplace.

At four o'clock, the king clapped his hands. "Robert-Houdin! Are you ready? Let the show begin!"

The magician bowed. "May I borrow six white handkerchiefs from the men in the audience?"

He tied a red ribbon around all six handkerchiefs. Then he placed them under the cover on the side table.

"I will make the handkerchiefs disappear," Robert-Houdin said. "But before I do, I want you to tell me something. Where would you like them to appear again? You choose the place."

He stepped from the stage and passed out pencils and cards. "On these cards," he said, "write where you want the handkerchiefs to be found."

Each person wrote on a card. Then Robert-Houdin took the cards.

"Sir," he said to the king. "Please pick three cards in a row."

Louis Philippe took three cards.

"Read the places written on the cards. Pick one place. That is where the handkerchiefs will appear."

The king read the first card. "On the stage, under the candle holder on the fireplace." He shook his head. "No, Robert-Houdin. Much too close for a smart magician like you."

He read the second card. "In the Dome of the Invalides" (an-vah-LEED). This was a famous church in Paris. "Too far away," the king said.

He read the third card. "In the box of the last orange tree in the garden."

In the palace garden, orange trees grew in wooden boxes.

"Yes," the king said. "That is a good place. Make your handkerchiefs turn up there."

He called a servant. "William! Go to the last orange tree. Make sure no one comes near it."

He turned to Robert-Houdin. "Let us see if your magic can help you. No one can get near the orange tree without being seen!"

Robert-Houdin went back on the stage. He lifted the glass cover on the side table. He held up the handkerchiefs tied with the red ribbon. "Here are the handkerchiefs." He carried the cover and the handkerchiefs to the center table. He placed the cover over them again.

"One—two—three! Behold!"

He lifted the cover. Out flew a white dove! The handkerchiefs? Gone!

The people gasped, "Ohh!"

"Sir," Robert-Houdin said to Louis Philippe, "kindly ask William to look in the orange-tree box. Tell him to bring what he finds."

In a few moments, the servant walked up to the king. "Sir, we found this in the roots of the orange tree." He held a rusty iron box.

The king said, "Robert-Houdin! Is this some of your foolishness? How can I open this box? It is locked!"

Robert-Houdin called the dove. It was sitting on the fireplace. It flew to his finger. Around its neck was a gold key. The magician asked the king to take the key and open the lock.

Inside the box was a sheet of yellow paper and a small package. A red ribbon was tied around the package. The king read the words on the paper.

> On this day, the 6th of June, 1786 an iron box was placed in the roots of an orange tree by me, Balsamo, Count of Cagliostro.
> It will serve in an act of magic. This magic will take place 60 years from today before King Louis Philippe of France.

Cagliostro (kal-YOE-stroe) was a famous magician. He had died 51 years before.

The king broke the ribbon on the package. He took off the paper. Inside were the missing handkerchiefs!

How did Robert-Houdin make the handkerchiefs show up in the iron box? This was the very place the king picked for them to appear. And the old letter. How did it get with the handkerchiefs? Where was Emile? What part did he play in the trick?

Magicians today say Robert-Houdin's "The Iron Box in the Orange Tree" is one of the great mysteries in magic. Can you possibly guess how Robert-Houdin did it? For the solution, turn to page 63.

The Last Trick

"There are many good magicians," Howard Thurston once said. "But there are few good assistants."

All magicians need assistants, or helpers, to put on a magic show.

The best known of all assistants was George White. He began working with Thurston when he was only 9 years old. For the next 37 years, he traveled with Thurston. They gave shows all over America and in many other countries.

"I have never given a show without George White," Thurston said. "And I never will. Without George, my show can't go on." Thurston and White were proud to work together. They needed each other.

George White helped Thurston with the

tricks he used in
the show. Thurston
cut a woman in half with a saw. He changed
a marble statue into a living woman. He
made playing cards appear in the air.

And White always helped Thurston with
the great trick that ended the show.

When people came into the theater, they
saw a large black box. The box was above
them near the ceiling. It hung by a rope.
The rope ran down to one corner of the
stage.

People wondered what the box was for. They kept on wondering all through the show.

Then finally Thurston and White pulled a large cannon onto the stage. Thurston borrowed a handkerchief from a man in the audience.

A pretty, young woman walked onto the stage. Thurston tied the handkerchief around her arm.

The woman smiled and waved to the audience. Then she climbed into the cannon. The band began to play.

George White pointed the cannon toward the box high above the people. He lighted a match. He held it up so the people could see it. "I'm ready when you are!" he said to Thurston.

The band stopped playing. Thurston counted: "One . . . two . . . three! Fire!"

White touched the match to the back of the cannon. BOOM! A great blast shook the theater. Smoke poured from the cannon. Then White opened the back of the cannon. People could see right through it. The woman was gone!

"As you can see," Thurston said, "our lovely young lady has left us. Now let us see if we can find her."

He pointed to the side of the stage. White untied the rope that ran up to the box. Slowly the box came down to the stage. He and Thurston carried the box to the center of the stage.

Thurston opened the top of the box. What was inside? A second, smaller box. He and White lifted it out. Thurston opened the second box. A THIRD box was inside. He and White lifted this box out, too.

Thurston opened it. Out stepped THE WOMAN WHO HAD CLIMBED INTO THE CANNON! Again she smiled and waved.

Thurston took the handkerchief from her arm and returned it to the owner. "Thank you for the loan of your handkerchief."

The people whispered to each other.

"Why wasn't the woman blown apart when the cannon fired?"

"Maybe she has a twin sister."

"No, that can't be. She stepped out of the box still wearing the handkerchief. It was the same one she had on when she stepped into the cannon."

George White stood at one side of the stage. He watched the people. He smiled a slow smile. No one knew how he and Thurston had shot the woman from the cannon on the stage to the box on the ceiling.

Do you know how they did it? See if your answer is the same as the one on page 67.

Solutions

The Indian Basket Trick

Remember when the magician pulled the cloth away from the basket?

Just before that the boy inside opened the cover. Hidden by the cloth, he slipped out of the basket. The magician SLOWLY pulled the cloth away. He wrapped it around his waist. All the while, the cloth hid the boy. The people could not see him. The boy climbed onto a rope loop that hung between the magician's legs.

When the magician plunged the sword into the basket, the boy screamed. The people THOUGHT the screams came from inside the basket.

Then the magician opened the basket. The people came close to look inside. Raymond did, too. While everyone was looking into the basket, the boy slid out from under the magician's skirt. He climbed the tree.

The blood on the sword? That was red ink! A sponge soaked in red ink was inside the cover of the basket. People could not see it there.

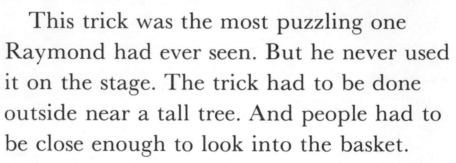

The third time the magician plunged the sword into the basket, the sword went into the sponge. It came out dripping with red ink. People BELIEVED that they saw blood.

This trick was the most puzzling one Raymond had ever seen. But he never used it on the stage. The trick had to be done outside near a tall tree. And people had to be close enough to look into the basket.

But the trick was not wasted. From it Raymond learned something very important. He learned that there can be great magicians in far-off countries and of different colors who do amazing things.

The Trickiest Trick

Houdini "walked through a brick wall" two times a day for three weeks. And every day a magician from the Society of American Magicians watched him. Finally, the members guessed how he did it.

There was only one way for Houdini to get from one side of the wall to the other. He had to go UNDER the wall.

After Houdini stepped inside the screen, he closed it around him. Then he tapped the rug.

Below the stage, a helper heard the tap. It was a signal to open a trap door. The door was in the floor of the stage. The wall stood on the rug over the trap door. The rug hid the trap door from the people on the stage.

When the trap door opened, the rug sagged a little. This made an open space under the beam. Houdini needed only a few seconds to finish the trick. He quickly slid under the beam. He stood up on the other side of the wall. The second screen hid him. Again he tapped his foot. Below the stage, the helper closed the door. This pushed the rug back into place.

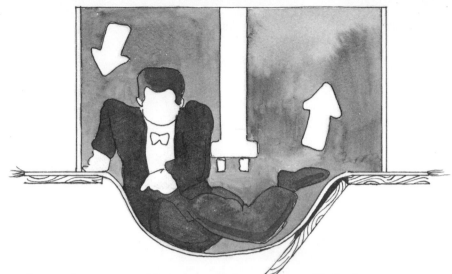

People standing on the rug didn't see or feel it move. So they didn't think about a trap door. Even the magicians took three weeks before they guessed how Houdini did it. People in the audience never guessed the secret.

In September 1914, a magic store in New York put up a sign:

THE SECRET TO

WALKING THROUGH A BRICK WALL.

YOU CAN DO IT, TOO!

PRICE: ONE DOLLAR!

Houdini never used the trick again. He didn't have to. For three weeks, he had fooled everyone, even other magicians. That was reward enough.

The Chinese Wizard

How did Chung Ling Soo catch goldfish in the air?

The answer came from two places. 1. The BAIT on the end of the fishing line. 2. The HANDLE of the fishing pole.

People thought the bait was a worm. But it was really a hollow metal tube. Inside was a piece of shiny orange cloth. The cloth was cut to look like a goldfish. When Chung Ling Soo swung the rod up, the cloth fish came out of the tube. The magician twisted

and turned it in the light. It looked just
like a real goldfish.

Then Chung Ling Soo swung in the cloth
fish. As he grabbed it, he turned the handle
of the fishing rod. The handle was hollow. It
was made up of short sections. Each section
was packed with wet cotton. In the cotton
was a goldfish. The water in the cotton kept
the fish alive.

As Chung Ling Soo turned the handle, a
section opened. A live goldfish dropped into
his left hand. He took the cloth fish off the
line. Then he dropped the cloth fish and the
real fish into the bowl. The real fish swam
around. The cloth fish sank to the bottom.

Where did the bowl come from? Chung Ling Soo carried it onto the stage under his long robe. It hung between his knees from straps around his hips. The people could not see it. Remember when he held the cloth near the stage? At that moment, he bent his knees and placed the bowl on the stage. The straps then let go of the bowl. He stepped back at the same moment he pulled the cloth away. There was the bowl for the people to see.

There was something else that people never caught on to. Chung Ling Soo was really William Robinson, an American magician.

Robinson grew up in New York City. He worked hard with his magic act. But few people came to see his show. In the year 1900, he started to call himself Chung Ling Soo. People thought a Chinese magician was special. He became popular in both America and Europe. People believed he was Chinese because he lived like a Chinese person. He had Chinese furniture in his home. He worked with Chinese helpers. On the street he dressed in Chinese robes.

Suee Seen was really Robinson's American wife, Dot. At one time, she was a dancer in musical shows. Now she also wore Chinese clothes and lived like a Chinese person.

The act lasted 18 years. No one ever guessed the answer to the goldfish-from-the-air trick. And no one ever guessed that Chung Ling Soo and Suee Seen were Mr. and Mrs. William Robinson from New York.

The Floating Princess

Did you say that "The Floating Princess" was a clever trick? You were right. Onstage beside Kellar, you would have seen how the trick worked.

The woman was really lying on a board on the sofa. Her hair and dress covered it. A black iron bar went from the board through an opening in the curtain. The audience could not see the bar.

A helper stood behind the curtain. When Kellar said "Up!" the helper pulled a rope.

The rope went over a wheel above the
helper's head. Then it went down to the bar.
The helper's pull lifted the bar, the board,
and the princess. It looked as if she were
floating in the air.

How could the hoop go along the
woman's body?

The iron bar was
bent in a long S curve.
When Kellar moved the
hoop from the woman's
head to her feet, the
hoop went into one
curve of the S.

When he came to her
feet, Kellar stopped.
He could not move
the hoop farther. Next
he moved the hoop
back to her head. He
took it off and walked
to her feet. There he
placed the hoop
around her feet and
walked it to her head.
The hoop went into
the other curve of the S.

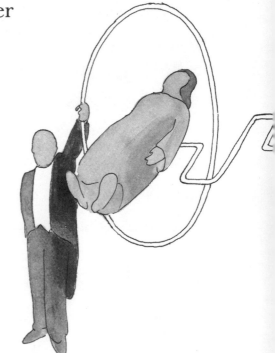

The audience thought the hoop passed all
along the princess. But it didn't.

Was Princess Karnac a real princess? No.
She was one of Kellar's helpers. Was she
hypnotized? Not at all. She enjoyed a little
rest.

With "The Floating Princess," the old "uncle" who didn't look like a magician fooled everyone. Did he fool YOU?

The Iron Box in the Orange Tree

Emile made the trick work.

To begin with, the top of the side table was hollow. Emile stood behind the side curtain. No one could see him. He reached into the hollow top and opened a tiny trap door. He took the six white handkerchiefs from under the cover. In their place, he put six new white handkerchiefs. The new handkerchiefs were tied with red ribbon.

Emile wrapped the first set of handkerchiefs in paper. He placed the package and the letter from Cagliostro in the iron box. Before going to St. Cloud, Robert-Houdin had written the letter on old paper.

While the people were writing the cards, Emile went to the last orange tree. He opened the box and dug out a little earth. He placed the box among the tree's roots. Now his part of the trick was done.

Meanwhile, Robert-Houdin was taking the cards from the people. When he had them all, he turned to take the cards to the king.

For a moment, his back was to the people. He slipped the real cards into an inside pocket of his suit coat. At the same time, he took out a second set of cards. In this set, each group of three cards was the same. The first card named the candle holder. The second card named the church. The third named the orange tree. The king THOUGHT the people in the audience had written these places. But Robert-Houdin had written the cards ahead of time.

He also knew which place the king would pick. The candle holder was too easy. The church was too far away. The box in the orange tree was just right. (Wouldn't YOU have picked the same place?)

The dove was in the center table. It was in a secret box under the top. Robert-Houdin placed the cover over the handkerchiefs. Then he pushed a hidden button. The button made a trap door open in the table top. The handkerchiefs dropped down. The dove popped up under the cover. The gold key was already around the bird's neck.

Everyone thought that Robert-Houdin had performed magic. No one saw that "The Iron Box in the Orange Tree" was a carefully planned trick.

From that time on, Robert-Houdin was known as the Master Magician of France.

The Last Trick

You may have already guessed something about this trick. The young woman was NEVER SHOT FROM THE CANNON.

Here is what happened.

She climbed into the cannon. Then she slid out through a secret opening. In the stage was a trap door. The audience could not see it. The woman went through the trap door. Under it was an open space. There she waited.

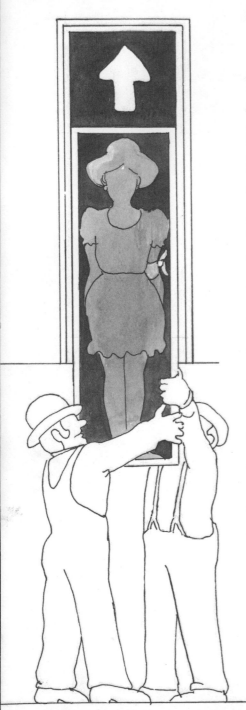

The cannon was pulled
off the stage. Then Thurston
and White placed the large
box over the trap door. The
box had a second box inside.
The woman was in a third
box under the stage. Helpers
under the stage pushed
the box up through the
trap door and into the first
two boxes. The bottoms of
these boxes were on hinges.
They swung in. When
Thurston opened the third
box, there she was! The
audience was amazed
to see her.

Thurston and White's 37 years together ended in 1936. That is when the great magician died. At Thurston's funeral, George White watched sadly as the magician's wand was broken. The broken wand meant that the show was over. The last trick was performed. There would be no more magic.

ABOUT THE AUTHOR

Robert Kraske has spent many years writing and editing magazine articles and books for children. Among other subjects, he has written about pirates, Harry Houdini (a famous magician), Benedict Arnold (an infamous Revolutionary War general), the patriotic songs we sing, the Statue of Liberty, burglar alarms, messages in seagoing bottles, and life in outer space. Mr. Kraske is also the author of the Step-Up Book, *Daredevils Do Amazing Things.* He lives in Stillwater, Minnesota, with his wife and three children.

ABOUT THE ILLUSTRATOR

Richard Bennett, a former graphic designer, is presently a freelance illustrator whose delightful illustrations frequently appear on television and in books and magazines. This is the first full-length children's book he has illustrated.

Mr. Bennett is married and has two children, Kathleen and Paul. The Bennetts live in Crestwood, New York.